The Giving Christian

Sowing Seeds for an Eternal Harvest

KIRK NOWERY

Published by Spire Resources, Inc.
PO Box 180, Camarillo, CA 93011
1-800-992-3060

Cover and text design by Bill Thielker

Printed in the United States of America

ISBN 0-9715828-9-0

CONTENTS

To Ashley, Clint and Matt

Three of the greatest
gifts I have ever received
and
three of the greatest givers
I have ever known.

C.S. Lewis, the eminent English scholar, said this about Christian giving:

The limit of giving is to be the limit of our ability to give.

For me, that statement is a perfect fit with this book because these pages deal with the full spectrum of giving. This isn't just about giving money to the church. It's about everything that we're capable of giving as human beings and followers of Christ, realizing that what we give and how we give define to a great extent who we are.

Perhaps you've heard someone say, "He's just a taker." Or, on the other hand, you've heard, "She is such a giver." Those two labels—*taker* and *giver*—actually need no embellishment. We understand exactly what they mean, and we picture in our minds precisely the kind of person who fits into each category. The taker goes through life thinking that he or she deserves and has a right to everything that can possibly be acquired. They're like the human version of the squirrel who has taken so many acorns, its face is puffed out to twice the normal size. The giver, on the other hand, practices the biblical truth that "it is more blessed to give than to receive."

There's an interesting fact about the Scripture verse I just quoted. Although it is a statement of Jesus Christ, you won't find it in any of the four Gospels. It appears only in the book of Acts, in the Apostle Paul's heart-wrenching farewell to the elders of Ephesus. The full passage reads like this: "I [Paul] have not coveted anyone's silver or gold or clothing. You yourselves know that these hands of mine have supplied my own needs and the needs of my companions. In everything I did, I showed you that by this kind of hard work we must help the weak, remembering the words the Lord Jesus himself said: 'It is more blessed to give than to receive.'"[1]

Paul was a giver. From the moment of his spiritual transformation on a dusty Judean road, he was constantly giving to others—giving them God's truth, giving help, giving money, giving encouragement. Like his Master, Paul was not concerned about getting things, hoarding material wealth or achieving personal prestige. He just wanted to give. We can try to make it more complex, but it's actually quite simple.

I'm guessing that, like me, you want to be known as a giver, not a taker. You want your life to count, to have a value that is not measured in dollars and cents but in the currency of heaven. In that sense, you want to be rich, spiritually rich; but the way to acquire that wealth is through giving, not taking.

In this book you're going to meet some interesting people and read some fascinating stories. But, most of all, you're going to encounter some life-changing truths about what it means to be a Giving Christian. I pray that these words will make a lasting difference in your life.

1

GIVING THE GIFT OF TRUTH

Sharing the Reason for Your Hope

Bono.

His name instantly conjures images of a larger-than-life personality, the brightest light in a constellation of rock stars. But Bono, lead vocalist for U2 and unabashed activist, is surprisingly different from the flashy image. Behind his ever-present sunglasses are eyes that see the world clearly and a mind that grasps spiritual realities. In the compelling book, *Bono: In Conversation With Michka Assayas,* he was asked about his faith. Bono said, "I'd be in big trouble if Karma was going to finally be my judge. It doesn't excuse my mistakes, but I'm holding out for Grace. I'm holding out that Jesus took my sins onto the

"It's not our own good works that get us through the gates of Heaven."

Cross, because I know who I am, and I hope I don't have to depend on my own religiosity."

Assayas replied, "The Son of God who takes away the sins of the world. I wish I could believe in that." To which Bono answered, "...The point of the death of Christ is that Christ took on the sins of the world, so that what we put out did not come back to us, and that our sinful nature does not reap the obvious death. It's not our own good works that get us through the gates of Heaven."[1]

The journalist, true to his profession, was trying to get something out of Bono—a bold statement, a shocking admission or a juicy comment. What he was given was perhaps bolder and more shocking than he had anticipated. A world-famous musician had just given him the Gospel. Who would ever expect that? Who would ever think that a man who personifies hipness would talk so seamlessly about grace, about atonement, about the deity of Jesus Christ? But he did, because he was ready to share passionately the truth that sets humans free.

Bono was practicing an ancient principle. It was expressed this way by one writer in 63 A.D.: "In your hearts set apart Christ as Lord. Always be prepared to give an answer to everyone who asks you to give the reason for the hope that you have."[2] Bono was prepared to give the reason for his hope in Christ, and that's precisely what he did. Had he given the journalist a million dollars (which he could easily do), it would have been worth nothing in comparison to the truth he communicated.

A lot of people have a hard time believing that there is truth to be found. Many are burned by bad experiences or let down by life in some way, and they're left with scars and suspicions. Others are turned off by the very idea of absolute truth. They just can't see how one truth would be exclusive and transcendent above all the rest. It just doesn't seem to show "tolerance."

A friend of mine was passing through a train station when a bit of graffiti caught his eye. An evangelistic vandal had scrawled,

Christ is the answer.

Underneath those words, in a different script, a second tagger had written,

What's the question?

And beneath that, a third philosopher had added a final commentary,

Life is the question.

Three people, less than a dozen words, but a profound "discussion" about a subject that touches every human being. If Christ *is* the answer—the answer to life itself—then there's no getting around the implications. If I don't connect with Him in some definitive way, how can I hope to experience life in the fullest sense? If I'm to believe C. S. Lewis, Jesus made some claims that are either outrageously wrong or categorically right.

Lewis, of course, goes with the latter. And so do I.

If Christ is the answer—the answer to life itself—then there's no getting around the implications.

When I look at what Jesus actually said, though He spoke the words twenty centuries ago, I get goosebumps of amazement. In the days just before His passion, Jesus was meeting with a group of His followers, encouraging them to look hopefully to the future. "Do not let your hearts be troubled," He told them, "...You know the way to the place where I am going." Thomas—the infamously "doubting" Thomas—blurted out, "Lord, we don't know where you are going, so how can we know the way?" And in the most categorical, leave-no-doubts manner, Jesus replied, "I am the way and the truth and the life. No one comes to the Father except through me."[3] *Yes*, He was saying to Thomas and the others, *Yes, you do know the way because you know me.*

There is no room for compromise or halfway positions. What He said places every human being on one side or the other.

When Jesus was brought before the Roman governor Pontius Pilate, He told him, "You are right in saying I am a king. In fact, for this reason I was born, and for this I came into the world, to testify to the truth. Everyone on the side of truth listens to me." Pilate, either thoroughly confused or profoundly convicted replied, "What is truth?"[4]

Everyone on the side of truth listens to me. Wow, what a statement! That's as categorical and straightforward as you can get. But Jesus said it, and we have to deal with it. There is no room for compromise or halfway positions: what He said places every human being on one side or the other. That's why He boldly said, "He who is not with me is against me."[5]

The biblical record tells us explicitly that truth is wrapped up in a Person—in who Jesus was, what He said and what He did. Look at any calendar and you'll see that His life is the dividing line in history. It is also the dividing line in every human heart. To find Him is to find the way, to know Him is to know the truth, to have Him is to have life itself. The Gospel—literally, the Good News—is the message of His redeeming, sacrificial love. In receiving and believing that message, trusting only in Him, a person receives the "gift of God"[6]—eternal life.

Whenever I meet a famous person—and I've had the opportunity to meet several—I find myself talking about that person, whoever it is, for several days afterwards. Perhaps you've had that same experience. It's as if some kind of energy has been transmitted and you keep thinking about that person and you're keenly aware of their fame, fortune or importance. You don't have to work up the courage to mention your "connection" with whomever the person is. You simply talk openly and eagerly.

When I think about the fact that, spiritually speaking, I personally know the most important figure

The essence of giving truth is giving Christ.

in all of history, it makes me shake my head in astonishment. It also makes me realize that I should talk naturally and freely about my relationship to Jesus Christ—as freely as I would talk if I had just met the President of the United States. The difference is that I'm not really in a position to introduce anyone to the President, but I am in a position to introduce another person to Jesus Christ.

The essence of giving truth is giving Christ. When I communicate to someone His story, His message and His relevance, I am communicating truth. It isn't truth because I said it is, but because He said so. *I am the truth* He declared. So, for the Giving Christian, the pressing question is: How can I clearly and most effectively communicate truth by giving Christ to another person? Or, to put it another way, How can I give the reason for my hope?

The simplest advice I can give is this: If you have believed in Jesus Christ alone, if you have received God's gift of eternal life through Him, then determine to get to know Him in a spiritually intimate way. Think about Him. Communicate with Him daily, even moment to moment, in prayer. Read His words, meditating on them and memorizing them, not out of ritual, but out of love.

Years ago when I first met my wife, Denise, whenever we were apart and I would get a letter from her, I would cherish it to the point that I would know the words by heart, even though I never consciously attempted to memorize them. That's the way it is with love. If you're in love, you value every communication with your loved one, you prize that person's words, and your intimacy deepens because of it.

It's become easier and easier for me to talk about my faith in Jesus Christ. I've learned to not think of it as some kind of religious duty to perform or obligation to fulfill. Christ has transformed my life and given me purpose. So, to talk about Him is simply a matter of communicating the significance of that

He is the reason for my hope, and He's the source of my freedom. He is truth and that truth has set me free.

transformation. He's the reason for my hope and the source of my freedom. He is truth, and that truth has set me free.

After the historic Emancipation Proclamation of 1863, Abraham Lincoln was meeting with a group of newly-freed slaves when one of the men knelt at Lincoln's feet to thank him. The President reached down, took the man's hand and brought him to his feet. "Please don't bow to me," said Lincoln, "I'm a man just like you, and we both should bow only to the One who created us and truly gives us our freedom." Old Abe had a keen understanding of truth. He could look into the face of a former slave and know that in God's eyes they were no different, that they were both in need of the freedom that only He can give.

Has the truth set you free? Then talk about it. Give that truth to the people you meet on life's pathway. Let them know the reason for your hope!

2

GIVING THE GIFT OF HELP

Caring for People in Need

You've undoubtedly heard of Mother Teresa. But chances are you've never heard of "Father" Thomas. Yet millions of people across the Indian subcontinent believe that his life has made an impact equal to the revered nun of Calcutta. M. A. Thomas is "Father" to over 10,000 children from the poorest of India's poor—orphaned and abandoned children that no one cared for until he rescued them from unspeakable deprivation. To each one he has given food and clothing and a roof over their heads and—above all—a boundless love.

In 1960, having just graduated from college in Madras, M. A. Thomas had only 200 rupees to his name—the equivalent of just $8—and virtually no earthly possessions. But in his heart was an inexpressibly great treasure that he was eager to share—a deep, genuine desire to help everyone that God would enable him to help. With his wife Ammini, then pregnant with their first child,

M. A. Thomas had only 200 rupees to his name—the equivalent of just $8—and virtually no earthly possessions.

M. A. was ready to set off by foot for the Indian state of Rajasthan—1,500 kilometers away. They were headed there because it was considered the most spiritually challenging and needy place in all of India. The young couple was prepared to walk an extraordinary distance to a place they had never seen, without the promise of a job or a place to stay. However, a few days before they were to begin their journey, they met a distinguished visitor from the United States, a man named Bill Bright. Dr. Bright, founder of the worldwide Christian ministry, Campus Crusade, heard M. A.'s testimony and was impressed with such remarkable determination. He took $25 from his own pocket and gave it to M. A., with the promise that he would continue to send at least that much every month in missionary support. (Incidentally, Bill Bright kept his promise, sending monthly ministry gifts until his death in 2003).

Using a portion of that first gift of $25, M. A. was able to purchase train tickets to Rajasthan. Though he and Ammini were ready to walk, it would not be necessary, after all. But they had no idea what lay ahead. Arriving in Kota, Rajasthan, on a blistering August day in 1960, M. A. went to the most prominent intersection and began to preach the Gospel. He was promptly arrested, jailed, beaten and ordered by the magistrate to leave the city. After his release, M. A. went back to the same intersection and began to

M. A. was ready to set off by foot for Rajasthan—1,500 kilometers away.

preach the same message! Again, he was arrested, but his joyous attitude confounded the authorities. "Why are you here? And why won't you leave?" the judge demanded to know. Thomas replied, "I'm here to tell the Good News to everyone, and I can't leave because God sent me here to help those for whom no one cares." The judge was intrigued. "What is this 'good news' you have?" he asked. M. A. then shared Christ's message of hope and salvation. The judge was interested, but first he wanted to know why anyone would be interested in the poor. "Because Jesus loved the poor and the disadvantaged, I love them, too," he answered. In a culture where cows are valued more highly than the lives of some human beings, it was a radical thing to say. Reluctantly, the judge jailed M. A. for the night, but he rescinded the order that he leave the city.

Today, over four decades later, M. A. Thomas is the most beloved man in Kota, a city of two million souls. He has never stopped preaching the Good News or daring to touch the "untouchables" of society. Over the years, M. A. has dealt with countless crises and challenges; but along the way he has founded a college, trained thousands of ministers, built a hospital and numerous clinics, created a network of schools, and established nearly a hundred children's homes across the length and breadth of India. In the city of Kota is Emmanuel Children's Home, the first orphanage established by M. A. Thomas. Today it is a community of more than 1,500 boys and girls who otherwise wouldn't know the satisfaction of a good meal, the security of a safe home, or the joy of a loving embrace. But they know all that and more because years ago one man decided that he would be a giver— a giver of help to the helpless, a giver of hope to the hopeless.

One life can make such an amazing difference! I look at the example of M. A. Thomas and think, *I want to make a difference like he has.* I see in him a man who has never had a lot of money, who still lives in a small apartment and who doesn't care about *things.* What he cares about is *people.* He is motivated every day to give, and that simple fact speaks volumes to me. You cannot make a difference in this life unless you're a giver. Takers—those who go through life claiming and keeping all they can—are, in the final analysis, just losers. Only givers are the truly successful, the truly effective.

Giving help implies many things because help comes in many forms. Help can take the shape of financial contribution, personal advice, physical assistance or emotional comfort, just to name a few examples. The Giving Christian understands the essential nature of help, that it is the practical application of a spiritual discipline. Along life's road, time after time, we are called upon to be a friend to the friendless, a counselor to the confused, a peacemaker for the troubled, or a guide to the lost. Only the person who has made a spiritual decision to be

The Giving Christian understands the essential nature of help, that it is the practical application of a spiritual discipline.

God provides the ever-present power of His Spirit to guide you to success, and with His enablement you can be a significant influence in others' lives.

a giver will make the most of those opportunities.

Being a giver of help demands mastery of your words, your actions, your reactions and your attitudes. Of course, only you can control what you say, what you do and how you respond in life's constantly changing circumstances. Fortunately, you don't have to handle this challenge alone. God provides the ever-present power of His Spirit to guide you to true success, and with His enablement you can be a significant influence in others' lives.

Be aware. For the giver, it is imperative to be aware and sensitive to what others are thinking, feeling and experiencing. Insensitivity—willfully ignoring or disregarding other people—spoils a God-given privilege to show His love and demonstrate His character. God is kind, and His heart's desire is that we be kind, too. One "fruit of the Spirit"[1] is kindness—the gentle, caring attitude that motivates us to act compassionately toward others. It is the attitude we see in Jesus throughout the New Testament. He was attuned to the needs of people, and His kindness was strong and undeniable, always reaching out to oppressed and burdened souls around Him. He was God in human flesh, worthy of worship; yet He lowered Himself to be a kind, selfless servant.

Be tough. When you're giving help, don't pull punches when a situation calls for directness. Jesus spoke so directly and forcefully that many people who desperately needed His help rejected Him. "His sayings are too hard,"[2] they said. Speak the truth in love[3], the Bible advises us. If you're reaching out to help someone (especially a friend) who is engaged in self-destructive behavior, don't make excuses for them or make things too easy for them. Giving help does not mean giving in.

Be tender. Frankly, it is often easier to be tough and strict than to be tender and kind. It can take a real effort to have patience and understanding with some people; but it can have a transformational effect. I was touched years ago in reading the story of Tom Anderson, who had brutally murdered another man. Tom was visited in prison by his victim's mother, who came to him with a simple, specific message. Some time had passed since the crime, and God had comforted her heart. She went to the prison to tell Anderson that God loved him in spite of his horrendous sin and that he could find forgiveness in Jesus Christ. She then told him that her special message could be summed up in just three words: "I forgive you." They were such simple words, yet they overwhelmed him. After her visit, Tom prayed to God and begged for the forgiveness she had described and the kindness she had shown. There in that maximum-security prison, he was spiritually liberated, changed by the power of Christ. His life was radically affected because a woman who had every reason to despise him, had instead reached out to give help.

Be intentional. To be intentional is to take the initiative, to intercede with help even when you sense it may not be welcome. One of the greatest regrets of my life was a failure to stay connected with my brother-in-law, Dean. He had always been the sort of guy whose smile could light up a

To be intentional is to take the initiative, to intercede with help even when you sense it may not be welcome.

room, with a voice that could be heard above all others, and a personality without limits. But Dean had a troubled soul, haunted with who knows what kind of torment. I wish I had been more aware of the pain he was experiencing, but I was so busy ministering to thousands that I missed one in my own family.

One night a few years ago, Dean lost all hope and gave up on his ability to sustain his life. He made his family a great dinner, left a personal note for each one, then went to his office and took his own life. I was on the road when I got the call from my wife. I can still hear her crying, and I can still feel the convulsed emotions. It has left a hole in our souls. Apparently we had not been sufficiently aware of his struggles, nor intentional enough in reaching out to give help to Dean when he really needed it. He may have rejected us, but that's the risk that comes to the help giver.

Our family is comforted by the fact that Dean had openly expressed his faith in Christ. We will see him again in heaven one day. But the loss of Dean has made me resolve to never again close my eyes or cover my ears to the need of someone I am in a position to help. It's as if God is saying to me, *Kirk, whatever someone needs, even if you have to take them on your back and carry them, that's what it means to give help.*

> *The loss of Dean has made me resolve to never again close my eyes or cover my ears to the need of someone I am able to help.*

As Christians we are compelled to give help, not out of guilt but out of compassion.

29

Our English word *compassion* is derived from two Latin words which literally mean, "to suffer with." To have compassion is "to suffer with" other people—to put yourself in their shoes, to feel what they feel, to endure what they endure. This is what Jesus did constantly. So great was His love and concern that He was often "moved with compassion."[4] Throughout His earthly ministry He unceasingly gave help and healing to the poor, the diseased and the needy.

God is pleased when we do what Jesus did, giving compassionate help to those who are less fortunate. James 1:27 says that "Religion that God our Father accepts as pure and faultless is this: to look after orphans and widows in their distress." Giving to those who can give nothing back is a spiritually beautiful thing, and it honors God. In Acts 10, in the account of the Roman centurion Cornelius, the Bible says that "he gave generously to those in need and prayed to God regularly." In a vision from God, an angel told him, "Your prayers and gifts to the poor have come up as a memorial offering before God."[5] As a Christian, when you give help to and for others, it is the same as giving directly to God.

We must not look the other way when opportunities come. As Christ's followers we cannot insist upon clean hands and safe risks when our world is such an ugly and unlovely place for so many suffering people.

At dinner recently our waitress was an impressive young lady named Emily—impressive because her face seemed to glow and her personality was so memorable. We struck up a conversation and learned that she waited on tables to make a living, but her life—her mission—is to care for the "ladies of the night" in inner city Atlanta. She said, "when I leave here, I'm going to a neighborhood where 13-year-old girls literally sell themselves. I offer help and food and compassion in the name of Christ." In meeting Emily I was reminded that many of us need to stop praying for opportunities and take the ones that are already there.

Let's get our hands dirty, let's get out of our comfort zones, and—for the sake of Jesus Christ—let's show that we care. Whether it's an elderly person in grave need, a dying AIDS patient, a widow with little in earthly goods, or someone else in some other circumstance, what matters is that we act decisively in Jesus' name. When we give others help, we give Him honor.

3

GIVING THE GIFT OF SERVICE
Devoting Your Days to Christ

S omething just happened, something so abrupt and mind-jarring that it has taken the place of what I originally wrote for this chapter on "Giving the Gift of Service." Right now, Denise and I are overcome with emotion, struggling to keep our heads above waters that have surged in like a flood of feelings. Floating by are the relics of life—memories of years raising three wonderful children.

Two of those children are about to embark on an uncertain journey, and we can't go with them. The story began just a few days ago when my wife awakened me about midnight to say that Franklin Graham was on the phone, calling from Alaska. He had just

The first hand to reach out to help should be from those who represent Jesus Christ.

learned from our mutual friend Jerry Prevo that my daughter, Ashley, and my younger son, Matthew, were interested in serving somewhere in the world in a significant ministry. Franklin asked if all of us could meet in a few days to discuss the possibilities. I said yes, having no idea what those possibilities would include.

Denise and I are remarkably blessed that all three of our children are unreservedly committed to serving Christ. Our son Clint and his wife, Angela, are full-time leaders in the youth ministry of NorthPoint Church here in Atlanta. Ashley and Matthew have also been involved in ministry, but recently both of them have been burdened to do something bolder and more substantive in their service. Extensive involvement in short-term missions has heightened their awareness of needs around the globe, preparing their hearts for more long-term cross-cultural experiences.

When we met with Franklin Graham at the headquarters of Samaritan's Purse in North Carolina, I marvelled at what God is doing through that ministry. From a mere handful of people just a few years ago, Samaritan's Purse has grown into one of the world's largest and most effective Christian organizations devoted to relief and development. Franklin has said, "When there is an overwhelming need or a major crisis in the world, the first hand to reach out to help should be from those who represent Jesus Christ."

Franklin spoke first to Ashley, asking about her dreams and desires. Ashley has a genuine joy and authenticity. She is a discerner, enabling her to feel someone's needs and with a God-anointed word speak right into another person's heart and soul. She chose to become a Nurse Practitioner instead of a Doctor, as she puts it, so she can care for the whole person both physically and spiritually. She says it gives her time with them. Desiring only the best of the best, she received her training at Vanderbilt Medical School.

Of all the nations in the world, he had to bring up Sudan! Sudan, a country that is enduring the greatest trauma and upheaval.

Upon her graduation she accepted a position at one of Atlanta's leading hospitals, where she has worked for the past two years. She told Franklin Graham that she wants to use her gifts and skills where they can make a significant difference. In reply, he began to describe the ministry of Samaritan's Purse in Sudan.

I will admit that when Franklin started talking about Sudan, my heart missed several beats. Of all the nations in the world, he had to bring up Sudan! Sudan, a country that is enduring perhaps the greatest trauma and upheaval on planet earth—a genocide of epic proportions as Muslims from the northern regions have killed over 1.5 million Christians in the south. Samaritan's Purse operates a hospital in Sudan, and most observers consider it the most important Christian outpost in a calamitous land.

Franklin told us about the hospital—a place where the medical staff must tend to landmine injuries, cases of malaria, machete wounds, and a never-ending line of patients suffering from tuberculosis and AIDS. "Ashley," he said, "just as the Good Samaritan didn't walk past, but tended to the one who was bruised and bleeding, I want you to wipe the wounds of those the world has forgotten and give them to Jesus. Please come to serve with us at the hospital in Sudan." I could tell from the expression on Ashley's face that her answer was *Yes*.

But Franklin wasn't done, of course. Then he began to converse with Matthew. And once again he talked about Sudan! I thought, *What's going on here? Matthew isn't trained in medicine!* But Franklin had another, very different kind of challenge in mind. "Matt," he said, "we have a huge project in the south of Sudan. We're rebuilding over 400 churches that have been burned during the war, and we're helping to replace the pastors of those churches because most of them have been killed. In fact, a great number of them were crucified—literally nailed to trees or to the walls of their churches." Franklin looked at my son and said, "Matthew, I want you to go and get me the name and story of every pastor and every church. I want you to find out how many people were burned inside those churches. I want those stories to be told so that no one will ever forget. Matthew, will you go?" Without one moment of hesitation, Matthew said, "I'm in!"

It was almost more than I could bear.

Thinking that we had heard it all, Franklin then told us the story behind the story. He said that over 80 years ago a pioneer missionary named Frazier had built the first hospital in Sudan and laid the foundation for the first missions work. For the first five years, Frazier had seen no fruit for his labors, and was spit upon daily by the tribesmen. He would simply wipe away the spit and keep on serving, caring for the sick and spreading the Good News of Jesus. After 20 years of excruciatingly hard work, he died. But before his death he told those whose lives had been changed that others would one day come to finish his work.

Before his death, he told those whose lives had been changed that others would one day come to finish his work.

When Samaritan's Purse went into Sudan several years ago, they discovered the old hospital. It had been nearly destroyed, with sections burned and landmines planted along the perimeter of the property. Another building that served as a church had been burned as well. Teams began to remove the landmines and rebuild the hospital and church, and in that place today is a thriving center of medical ministry.

"When we went in and began to work," Franklin said, "there were no tribespeople in the area. But soon after we started, some very old people came to us and said, 'We are so glad you are here. We have been waiting for you!' Not knowing what they were talking about, we asked, what for? They said, 'The missionary Frazier told us that one day you would come.' They had been waiting for us for more than 60 years!"

The power of that story reverberated for a few seconds of deafening silence. Without waiting for Ashley or Matthew to speak first, I said, "Franklin, my wife will ask you, 'What will be the level of safety for our children?'" At that moment, my kids laughed out loud. They spoke nearly in unison, "It isn't Mom, it's you asking that question, Dad." They were right, of course. I was feeling a heavy weight on my heart.

"If we're truly devoted to Christ, we can trust Him with... anything that comes our way."

Franklin looked at me, one father to another, and said words to this effect: "Kirk, our son graduated last year from West Point, and now he's in the Rangers. Right now he's deployed somewhere in the world; I don't know for sure where he is because he's not allowed to tell me. God has taught me through this that he is safer in a dangerous place in the center of God's will than he is anywhere else on earth. If we're truly devoted to Christ, we can trust Him with this and with anything else that comes our way."

After the meeting, making our way to the parking lot, everyone was silent. But as soon as we climbed into the truck to head back home, Matt turned to me and said once again, "I'm in. I've been waiting on a big opportunity from God, and this is it." For Ashley, as I knew all along, the answer was also an emphatic *Yes*. "This is what I have prepared and trained for. I have to go!" As I write these words, they are just a few weeks from departure for Sudan. By the time you read these words, God willing, they will already be serving there. And, tough as it is to grasp at times, I know that Franklin was right in saying they are safer there in the center of God's will than they are anywhere else. It doesn't mean that they won't encounter danger or suffer harm, but in His hand their security is eternal.

Into each life come opportunities for service, and those opportunities must be recognized and redeemed for God's glory.

If we're truly devoted to Christ, we can trust Him with this and with anything else that comes our way. Those words continue to encourage me as I think about what devotion means. Into each life come opportunities for service, and those opportunities must be recognized and redeemed for God's glory and His purposes. Writing on this subject, the Apostle Paul gave this counsel: "Be very careful, then, how you live—not as unwise but as wise, making the most of every opportunity, because the days are evil. Therefore do not be foolish, but understand what the Lord's will is."[1] Contrary to what many people would consider "common sense," Ashley and Matthew *are* being careful how they live—careful in that they are taking into account the will of God above all else. They are making the most of an opportunity for service to Christ.

I don't know what the pioneer missionary Frazier looked like, but I have in mind the image of a Livingstone-type character, slight of build but huge in determination—a determination exceeded only by his devotion. I am already imagining Matthew and Ashley serving in the same place where Frazier invested two arduous decades of his life. From the soil of Sudan the blood of the martyrs will cry out as my son gathers the stories of devoted saints who lived and died for the sake of Christ their Lord. And in a hospital where Jesus' mercy and love were first demonstrated generations ago, my daughter will redeem each day, loving the unlovely. For Matthew and for Ashley, as for you and me, giving devotion is what matters. The place where we are and the jobs we are doing are secondary to the first priority: serving Jesus Christ and putting Him above all else.

The Giving Christian is a giver of service and wholehearted devotion—not to a religious system or philosophy, but to a Person. Every act of service is an expression of worship for Him, a declaration of commitment to His will. That's why what each of us does in life matters: we're doing it for God, the One to whom we owe life itself.

Before you see Christ resurrected and victorious, remember the price that He paid—the shame, the scourging, the beating, the spit and the nakedness as He was nailed to those timbers. As He was tortured, as the beard was ripped from his face, as the nails were driven into his hands. See that and don't turn away, and then measure the word *devotion*. May we never forget that He, the giver of life itself, is the one to whom we devote our lives in giving the gift of service.

4

GIVING THE GIFT OF RESOURCES

Putting Your Money Where Your Heart Is

Peter Marshall, whose life was immortalized in the book and movie *A Man Called Peter*, had an uncanny ability to capture people's attention and cause them to think. On one occasion when he was pastor of Atlanta's Westminster Presbyterian Church, Dr. Marshall interrupted the worship service as the congregation was singing the old hymn, *Take My Life and Let It Be*. In the Gaelic brogue of his native Scotland, Marshall drew everyone's attention to the lyrics they were about to sing:

> *Take my silver and my gold—*
>
> *Not a mite would I withhold.*

Giving of our resources is a serious matter; but it's also a practice that brings inexpressible joy when done in the right spirit.

He explained the practical significance of "Not a mite would I withhold"—a reference to the widow's mite in the biblical story—and asked all who could not sing that line with absolute sincerity to not sing it at all. The instruments once again began to play, but the hundreds of voices that had been singing so energetically were completely silent. As the notes died down, Marshall stepped to the pulpit and made his final point: It's OK for this to make us stop and think because giving really matters and we must take it seriously.

He was right, of course. Giving of our resources *is* a serious matter; but it's also a practice that brings inexpressible joy and blessing when done in the right spirit. As Jesus said, "It is more blessed to give than to receive."[1] And, as Paul wrote in a letter to the Corinthians, "God loves a cheerful giver."[2]

Giving is at the heart of the Christian life, at the heart of the Gospel, and at the heart of God. "For God so loved the world that he *gave* his one and only son..."[3] God is the infinite and perfect Giver: giving is integral to who He is. And because giving is inherent in God's character, when we give we identify with Him and we reflect His likeness.

Everything of true value is given by God. He has given us life itself—physical life in the blood that courses through our human bodies and spiritual life in the blood of His Son, Jesus Christ, whose sacrifice makes possible our eternal salvation. God has set the pattern for giving, and there is no worthier goal than to give like He gives. But is that possible? It is not only possible; it is imperative.

As I've explored the Bible to find out what it means to be a Giving Christian, I have been reminded that giving has to do with much more than money. But it absolutely, positively *does* have to do with money. Let's be clear about that, and make no apologies for

Our *money,*
indeed all our
resources, don't really
belong to us.

that fact. I have heard for many years that giving the tithe is so "old school." But when I look at the Scriptures, it is evident that responsibility giving is foundational. It is the cornerstone on which sacrificial giving is built. Responsibility and sacrifice are, in fact, common to the practice of believers in both the Old Testament and New Testament eras.

As a pastor I initially found it uncomfortable to teach or preach on the subject of giving because I had not yet reached a point of personal conviction and commitment. I had seen giving as Christian value, similar to the importance of being a good husband, a good father, a hard worker, a dedicated witness for Christ. But I soon realized that being a giver demands both responsibility and sacrifice. I had to ask myself as a leader: Am I a responsible giver? Am I giving regularly, consistently and responsibly—before any ques-

tion of sacrificial giving is considered? I
you can't give sacrificially unless you'
responsibly, and that clearly meant the   ...ave
never seen an effective argument against the biblical
mandate for tithing. The Bible says, "If a man does
not provide for his own house, he is worse than an infi-
del."[4] And what about God's house? Haggai said, "Is
it a time to be living in your paneled houses while the
Lord's house remains a ruin?"[5] I was ultimately able to
say as a leader of my church and my home that giving—responsibly as well as sacrificially—is what God
desires of us as stewards. We must be found faithful!

Our money, indeed all of *our* resources, don't
really belong to us. They have been entrusted to us by
God to manage for His purposes. This is not simply an
opinion I have; it is a categorical expression of the
Scriptures: "The earth is the Lord's, and everything in
it."[6] The Giving Christian lives by a creed of stewardship, not ownership.

There is a great paradox here: I have the privilege

of giving, and I get the benefit and blessing of giving; but what I am giving is not actually mine—it belongs to God. Accepting that paradox liberates me from the bondage of trying to accumulate as much as I can in life or striving constantly to have bigger and better things than my neighbors.

Giving faithfully. Faithful givers are faithful stewards. In fact, the first and most important attribute of a steward is faithfulness. The Bible says emphatically: "It is required that those who have been given a trust must prove faithful."[7] The "trust" encompasses all the material resources given to us by God. His plan is that we manage those assets in a way that is spiritually wise and profitable.

There is a two-fold significance to giving faithfully. First, it means giving by faith in God, mindful that He is Lord of all. Second, it means giving in a faithful, dependable manner. In both meanings, God provides the power and we follow through with the practice. He puts faith in our hearts and we exercise that faith by giving for His glory to accomplish His purposes.

My years as a pastor convinced me that one who gives money faithfully is much more likely to faithfully give time and ability and other resources. Money is a major determinant of life, for as Jesus said, "Where your treasure is, there your heart will be also."[8] I've counseled with many people whose struggles and crises can be traced directly to their "treasure"—and consequently their heart—being in the wrong place. Faithfulness in giving—to the right purposes, in the right way—has a powerfully positive effect and keeps our priorities in order.

Money is a major determinant of life, for as Jesus said, "Where your treasure is, there your heart will be also."

Giving gracefully. The Apostle Paul asks a monumental question: "He who did not spare his own Son, but gave him up for us all—how will he not also, along with him, graciously give us all things?"[9]

Everything we have—everything—is a gift of God. I can think of anything in my life, small or large, no matter what it is, and tell you absolutely that I didn't earn it or deserve it. The house I live in, the car I drive, the clothes I wear, the money in my bank account—whatever it is, without exception, I have because God graciously gave it to me. In His infinite love, He smiled on me and blessed me—just as He does you.

So, when it comes down to how I am going to give, I must look first to the example of God. I see that He gives graciously, and I know that I am to give graciously, too. This means that I must never give in a way that magnifies my own magnanimity. Have you ever had someone give you a gift and then constantly remind you what a great gift they gave? Graceful giving never draws attention to itself, but directs attention to God.

Don't worry about how much you have or don't have to give. Instead, give in proportion to everything you have received.

Graceful giving seeks to glorify God, not to better one's own bottom line. And graceful giving is driven by a desire to lift up the recipient, not lift up the giver.

Giving proportionally. A powerful principle of stewardship is that God's provision dictates the believer's proportion. In other words, what He provides determines what we give. If He gives a little, from that little we are to give; if He gives abundantly, from that abundance we are to give. The measure of His giving determines the measure of our giving. As Jesus said, "To whom much is given, much is required."[10]

Don't worry about how much you have or don't have to give. Instead, give in proportion to everything you have received. My personal conviction is that giving begins with the tithe and extends beyond that to offerings for the Lord's work. The tithe is the simplest proportion to understand: it is 10% of the total. For me, it's easy to know what constitutes my tithe to the Lord's work: What does my W-2 say at the end of the year? What is one-tenth of that? Giving that amount

Exceptional needs require exceptional giving—giving beyond the baseline.

over the years has never had anything but a positive effect in my life. But the tenth is really just the baseline. Giving above and beyond that level moves the giver into exceptional or even sacrificial giving.

Relying upon the Lord and depending upon Him as our source, we grow in grace as we give. In the process, giving becomes a spiritually enlivening experience, for as we die to self we come alive in faith.

Giving sacrificially. In the first century after Christ, the young churches of Macedonia were persecuted severely and were materially poor, but in spite of their poverty they excelled in giving. Specifically, they gave to a ministry project that the Apostle Paul had initiated; and they gave in a most remarkable way: sacrificially, beyond their ability, willingly and eagerly—of themselves to God and of their resources to God's work. Here's how the Bible describes the giving

Christians of Macedonia: "Brothers, we want you to know about the grace that God has given the Macedonian churches. Out of the most severe trial, their overflowing joy and their extreme poverty welled up in rich generosity. For I testify that they gave as much as they were able, and even beyond their ability. Entirely on their own, they urgently pleaded with us for the privilege of sharing in this service to the saints. And they did not do as we expected, but they gave themselves first to the Lord and then to us in keeping with God's will."[11]

Study the great causes described in the Bible—like the cause to which the Macedonians gave, or the building projects for the Tabernacle and the Temple—and you'll see right away that they were funded through gifts above and beyond the tithe. Exceptional needs require exceptional giving—giving beyond the baseline, giving that is bold and generous and sacrificial.

Giving globally. The cause of Christ is an all-encompassing cause touching everyone and everywhere—to "the ends of the earth."[12] "For God so loved the *world*..."[13] The world of people, that is— every person of every era throughout history. "For God so loved the world that he *gave*..." God's love motivated Him to give, offering His own Son as our substitute and savior.

God loves and God gives globally, and this is our inspiration. The Giving Christian gives globally, earnestly supporting the worldwide work of Christ. The most spiritually vibrant believers I know are those who have a passion for world missions and who back up that passion with generous gifts to the Lord's work.

When Jesus sent out His disciples to declare the Gospel, He told them, "Freely you have received, freely give."[14] And that's what they did, freely giving all that they could in His name. Today, 20 centuries later, that is still the priority for us as followers of Christ—to faithfully, gracefully, proportionally and sacrificially sow the seeds of His truth throughout the world, knowing we will reap an eternal harvest.

5

GIVING THE GIFT OF STRENGTH

Encouraging Others to Prevail

Until the mid-point of the 20th century, no one had ever reached the top of Mt. Everest. The world's highest peak—at an altitude over 29,000 feet—had long been thought unconquerable. But on May 29, 1953, Edmund Hillary, a New Zealand beekeeper by occupation, did the unthinkable and became the first man to reach Everest's icy summit. Six weeks later, in honor of his historic achievement, he was knighted by Queen Elizabeth. In the years since his amazing accomplishment, Sir Edmund Hillary has been widely regarded as the world's greatest mountain climber.

Ed wasn't alone on the mountaintop that day. Someone else reached the summit of Everest with him—

But Ed wasn't alone on the mountaintop that day. Someone else reached the summit of Mt. Everest with him—someone who didn't receive the same acclaim and reward, but who accomplished as much or perhaps even more in getting there. Tenzing Norgay, a Nepalese shepherd who served as guide on the arduous ascent, had grown up in the shadows of Everest. For the Norgay family, the Himalayas were home and mountaineering was a way of life. For the British expeditionary team, Tenzing was the ideal choice, providing the perfect balance of practical experience and personal fitness. No one was more capable of giving strength to his fellow climbers, which he did without regard for his own fame or fortune. To his credit, Hillary has always acknowledged Norgay as his partner in history's most renowned climb. He is the first to say that Tenzing was the one who truly gave him strength, encouraging him, urging him on, convincing him to believe that they could make it to the top.

The successful ascent of Mt. Everest reminds me of an ancient biblical truth: "Two are better than one, because they have a good return for their work; If one falls down, his friend can help him up. But pity the man who falls and has no one to help him up!"[1] To be a Giving Christian is to be a giver of encouragement— literally, a giver of courageous strength. Over the course of your life, God will provide you with opportunities to give this kind of strength to other people. Not physical strength, but spiritual strength and stamina to keep going in the face of difficulties and challenges, to mend troubled relationships, to pursue noble dreams and desires.

Strength to never give up. Years ago, a man received some bad news—so bad that he sat down and cried when he heard it. His hometown had been devastated, left in shambles by an enemy force. Its protective barrier, a great wall, had been torn down and now lay in ruins. He was hundreds of miles away when the report reached him, and he felt as violated as his city. Something had to be done, and someone had to restore what had been destroyed. But, in an age long before rapid transportation, the task would not be easy.

Something had to be done, and someone had to restore what had been destroyed.

And first he would have to get some time off and permission to make the journey. Easier said than done, because he worked for the king of Persia, the most powerful man in the world at that time. The king's word on the matter would be final.

The desperate man's name was Nehemiah, and he is the subject of an entire book of the Bible. For every follower of Christ who desires both to have strength and to give strength, his story is an inspiration. At precisely the right moment, Nehemiah asked for the king's permission and received not only the go-ahead, but also all the supplies he would need for the task.

Soon he was bound for Jerusalem, ready to take on the rebuilding project of a lifetime.

Upon arriving in the holy city, Nehemiah found it to be indeed a pile of rubble. In spite of the presence of enemy forces, he scouted the entire area. Having made his preparations, Nehemiah went to his people and told them that he would lead the effort to rebuild the wall. His words gave them strength; his determination gave them courage. They rallied around this remarkable man and began to work. Over the next two months they faced opposition in the form of mockery, threats, treachery, rumors and even attempted murder. But, strengthened by their leader, they pressed forward and on the 52nd day the wall was completed. God's people had been emboldened, their enemies had been defeated and success was secured.

Nehemiah was a great leader, but he was an equally great encourager. He was strong, but he also gave strength. Following his example, others persevered. They prevailed against formidable obstacles and opposition because one man was burdened enough to take

Whatever the specific opportunity, God will give you specific strength and He will empower you to pass it on to others.

the initiative, to take on the challenge and to give strength to his people.

Your experiences may never be as dramatic as Nehemiah's, but the same God who led him is leading you. And, like him, you will have the opportunity to help others stand firm in the cruel face of obstacles and opposition. Perhaps you will be the one to give strength to a friend who just lost a job; or worse, lost a loved one. Perhaps you will be the counselor to a couple who are struggling to stay together. Perhaps you will be the encourager your church needs to move through a challenge rather than skirt by it. Whatever the specific opportunity, God will give you specific strength and He will empower you to pass it on to others.

Strength to look to Christ, not to self. Do you recall the biblical story of Peter attempting to walk on the water to get to Jesus? In the middle of the night, as the disciples were attempting to cross the Sea of Galilee in a tempestuous wind storm, Jesus came walking on the water towards them. They were terrified, of course. "It's a ghost!" they cried out. But Jesus said to them, "Take courage! It is I. Don't be afraid." Peter replied, "Lord, if it's you, tell me to come to you on the water." The Lord said, "Come," and Peter stepped into the water and began to walk toward Jesus. However, the Bible says that "when he saw the wind, he was afraid and, beginning to sink, cried out 'Lord, save me!'" Jesus reached out His hand and caught him. "'You of little faith, he said, why did you doubt?'"[2]

This story always reminds me to keep my focus in the right place. Peter quit looking at Jesus and looked instead at the wind, and by looking at the wind he was reminded of his own inadequacies. *I can't walk on water!* he told himself. And, as a consequence, he began to sink. I can tell you emphatically that the surest way to sink is to quit looking at Jesus. When I look at my own life and see my flaws, my weaknesses, my sins and my shortcomings, I feel them weighing me down. I just don't see how I measure up and I start to sink. But when I look to Jesus, I see him looking at me, just as He looked at Peter. And just as He told Peter to step out and experience the miraculous, so He directs me.

The lessons of this story (which I have to keep on learning), motivate me to encourage other believers, to tell them "Keep your eyes on Jesus!" When I train pastors and Christian workers, I counsel them that it is usually (not always, but usually) more effective to give strength than to give sympathy, to give power than to give pity. I advise them, tell people: "If you're climbing a mountainous challenge, look to Jesus at the summit. If you're running a demanding race, look to Jesus at the finish line. And if you're going through a tough experience that seems to require walking on water, look to Jesus, who reaches out and says, 'You can make it! Just keep your eyes on Me!'"

Strength to forgive and forget. At a recent speaking engagement I gave a talk on the subject of encouragement based on the biblical admonition to "provoke one another to good works."[3] I explained that the word "provoke" means to prod, to move along, to spur to action. This is what God wants us to do for one another—not to be nuisances but to be encouragers. "Some of you," I said, "have resisted doing something you know you should do—perhaps for a long, long time. Make the decision right now to change that. Obey the leading of God's Spirit and accept this 'prodding' as a gentle push in the right direction."

After I finished speaking a man walked up to me and told me he hadn't talked to his brother in more than 30 years! I asked him why and he said, "We said some harsh things to each other on a vacation when

It is usually more effective to give strength than to give sympathy, to give power than to give pity.

A man walked up to me and told me he hadn't talked to his brother in more than 30 years!

we were in our 20s, and we haven't talked since." This guy was now in his 60s! He welled up with tears as he told me the story and said it was just his pride that kept him from picking up the phone. I made him look me straight in the eye and promise that he would call his brother that day. That gray-haired man with a weathered face gulped hard and agreed he would do it. I gave him my cell number and told him to contact me with an update. Later that day he called to tell me he had called his brother, and when his brother answered and heard that familiar voice say "Hello," he broke down in tears. They would soon be meeting, the man told me, catching up on all the lost years.

I didn't do anything magical that day. I simply communicated the importance of doing what we know the Lord would have us to do—and in the process I helped that brother in Christ have the strength to follow through, willingly forgiving and forgetting. It's really that simple.

I encourage you to be a giver of strength to others. Don't be afraid to lovingly prod someone to do the right thing. Remember, God's instruction is not that we merely provoke, but that we "provoke one another to good works."

6

GIVING THE GIFT OF PRAYER

Interceding to Bless & Benefit Others

"He doesn't have a prayer."

That's what someone said about David as he lay comatose in intensive care, tubes protruding from his mouth and nose, intravenous lines running into his arms and legs, medical contraptions beeping and whirring on both sides of his bed.

"Actually," I was able to say, "he *does* have a prayer." In fact, I knew that David had a whole lot of prayers, because people were asking God to save his life. As the victim of a boating accident off the coast of Florida, he had been given little hope. But his

A prayer is a gift in the truest sense, because the blessing and benefit is focused on the recipient, not the giver.

mother believed, and she was the first to ask me to intercede on his behalf.

Thankfully, God did save David's life. The prayers were heard and answered affirmatively, and Dave is now living with renewed appreciation for each day. Loved ones, friends, and a great number of people who didn't even know him took the time to pray for his recovery. The crushing impact of his injuries was overcome by the persistent, faithful prayers of God's people.

One of the most beautiful, loving things we can do for other people is to pray for them. When we do, the result is always meaningful and sometimes miraculous. A prayer is a gift in the truest sense, because the blessing and benefit is focused on the recipient, not the giver. For the Giving Christian, the giving of prayers is a vital element of one's spiritual life. In technical terms, it's called *interces-sion*—the act of pleading for the sake of another person, making an appeal on their behalf. Intercession stands in contrast to the other forms of prayer we practice, most of which are centered on our own relationship to God. Petition, for example, is prayer

Intercession is prayer that moves us out of the realm of personal interest and into specific concern for specific people.

that asks God for His provision. Confession is prayer in which we confess our sins and failings to God. Adoration is prayerful worship, expressing praise for God's goodness and greatness, honoring Him simply for who He is. Thanksgiving is, clearly, giving thanks to God for His faithful supply of all we need, His gifts both seen and unseen.

Intercession is prayer that moves us out of the realm of personal interest and into specific concern for specific people. When we give the gift of intercessory prayer, we invite the power of God to act in another person's life. In doing so, we too are blessed. As we intercede, He intervenes; and His intervention can come through material provision, spiritual enablement, and emotional or physical healing. "Pray for each other," James wrote in his epistle, "so that you may be healed."[1]

Christians often glibly say to one another, "I'll be praying for you" without ever getting around to actually praying. I know this to be the case because I've done it so often myself! I need this reminder as much as anyone because I'm so prone to good intentions that never make it to the point of actual implementation. Admittedly, I'm encouraging myself as much in this chapter as I'm encouraging you! This is a truly important commitment, a practice that was perfectly modeled by Jesus Christ.

What we commonly call "The Lord's Prayer" is actually not the Lord's Prayer at all, but a sample prayer that Jesus gave to His disciples. The true Lord's Prayer is found in chapter 17 of John's Gospel, which is devoted entirely to the prayer of intercession Jesus prayed for His followers. By examining what He prayed for us, we can discover how to intercede for others, how to give the gift of prayer for their blessing and benefit. Let's take a closer look at a few choice words in the Lord's prayer in John 17...

"Now this is eternal life: that they may know you, the only true God, and Jesus Christ, whom you have sent." [2]

Pray that others may know God. Nothing in this temporal, earthly life is more important than knowing the key to the next life—the eternal, heavenly life to come. That key is knowledge—knowledge of "the only true God" and the one whom He sent, His Son Jesus Christ. This is not "head" knowledge we're talking about. It runs much deeper than merely

This is not "head" knowledge we're talking about. It runs much deeper than merely knowing about God intellectually.

knowing about God intellectually. One must also know Him experientially, personally committing to Him in a relationship of faith and fidelity.

As we pray for others to know God, these truths guide our intercession. Christian moms and dads, for example, intercede for their children, praying that their boys and girls will not just know about God, but truly know God. Christian bosses intercede for their employees; Christian employees intercede for their bosses as well as their colleagues, praying that those with whom they work will know God in truth. Caring Christians in all of life's relationships realize that the gift of prayer for one another is indeed valuable.

"Holy Father, protect them by
the power of your name..."[3]

"My prayer is not that you take them out of the
world but that you protect them from the evil one."[4]

Pray that others may be protected by God. This is a troubled, turbulent, dangerous world. It doesn't

Government and mili-tary forces can protect us, but the only reliable protection comes from another authority: from God Himself.

take even **60** seconds reading the headlines in the local paper or on the internet to realize that there are threats to our well-being and our security. Since 9/11 the risks have become such a concern that we now have a color scheme to indicate perceived levels of danger.

To a certain extent, governmental agencies and military forces can protect us, but the only reliable protection comes from another authority: from God Himself. Only in Him are we truly secure; only He provides genuine protection. And when Jesus prayed in His intercessory prayer, "Holy Father, protect them by the power of your name," He was referring to something deeper than physical protection. His plea is for the spiritual protection of believers in a world that is adamantly opposed to Christ and to all who follow Him.

From what do we need to be spiritually protected? I can think of several things: We need protection from the lure of this world's wealth. We need protection from the pull of pride. And we certainly need protection from the pursuit of pleasure. Materialism, pride and sinful pleasure are like magnets, forcefully attracting us to their sphere. That force can only be countered by another, stronger force—the power of God's name. God's desire is that we be in the world, but not of it; and while we are in it, to live with an "other-worldly" mindset. Wouldn't you love to know that people are praying for you in this way? What a gift this is to one another!

"I say these things...so that they may have the full measure of my joy within them."[5]

Pray that others will have true joy. Everyone wants to be happy. We're so focused on happiness as a society that we will do just about anything to get it. But happiness is completely relative to one's circumstances. If I'm faced with health problems, if I've just lost my job, if I don't have enough set aside for retirement, if, if, if... then it's likely I won't be happy. But joy is entirely different. Things can be going very badly, yet as a follower of Christ I can still have a heart full of joy in the bad times as well as the good.

One of the classics of Christian literature is a multi-volume set called *Foxe's Book of Martyrs*. Written by John Foxe back in the 1600s, the *Book of Martyrs* recounts the experiences of men and women who gave their lives in service to Jesus Christ. Their physical lives were ended with gruesome brutality; yet in so many of the accounts, they are reported as having died with a smile on the face, with words of forgiveness for their tormenters on their lips, even with laughter at the moment of death. In the face of unspeakable evil, they had joy! They weren't crazy or misguided or deluded in any way; their joy was deep and genuine because God had given it to them.

As you intercede for others, pray that they will have the "full measure" of Christ's joy, no matter what their circumstances may be. Pray that they will experience the settled satisfaction that He alone can give. Pray that their desire would not be just for happiness, but for the joy that transcends every personal struggle, every difficulty, every trial.

"Sanctify them by the truth; your word is truth." [6]

Pray that others will be spiritually dedicated. *Sanctify* is an old word that has a very special significance. It means to set apart for God and for His purposes—to be spiritually dedicated. When Jesus prayed that His followers would be sanctified by the truth, He was wanting them to know and obey the Word of God.

When you pray for others—whether they are family, friends, neighbors, pastors, teachers, fellow church member or even strangers—pray like Jesus prayed. Ask God to sanctify them by the truth. In other words, ask Him to use the truths of Scripture to purify and prepare their lives for effective Christian service. So often in my experience as a pastor and Christian leader I have been guided by a particular truth of the Bible, sometimes just a word or phrase, only to learn later that someone was praying that Scripture into my life. My life was enriched because someone was going to God on my behalf. That is humbling and challenging.

Never underestimate the importance of the time you spend praying for the spiritual dedication of another person.

> *"My prayer is not for them alone.*
> *I pray also for those who will believe in me*
> *through their message..."*[7]

Pray that others will be spiritually fruitful. Jesus was not praying only for His original followers. His intercession was "also for those who will believe in me through their message...." In that one important statement He enfolded every believer of every era since the moment of His ascension. That means He was praying for you and me! And just as those first followers were to be faithful in spreading the message of Christ, so are we to faithfully tell the Good News to our generation. The objective of the message we deliver is "that the world may believe" in Jesus Christ.

God's plan is to communicate His message through human beings. Prone as we are to stumbles and failings, we're still His chosen vessels, His messengers of grace. And for that we desperately need to pray for one another. Nothing is more spiritually invigorating than telling the message of Christ's love and salvation. But for some reason, nothing is more intimidating to so many Christians. Pray that those in the circle of your life who know Jesus Christ will be empowered and emboldened to share their faith. Pray that they will be effective messengers, clearly expressing the reason for their hope.

"May they be brought to complete unity to let the world know that you sent me and have loved them even as you have loved me."[8]

Pray that we will all experience true unity in Christ. The golden thread woven through the words of Jesus' prayer in John 17 is spiritual unity. Just as

Jesus and the Father are one, He prayed that His followers would also be one—united in spirit and purpose to do His will.

Just as Jesus and the Father are one, He prayed that His followers would also be one—united in spirit and purpose to do His will.

In unity there is strength, infinitely greater strength than we could ever experience independently. As we think of one another and pray for one another, may we never forget that we are united with God in Christ, and because of that union we have access to the Father. We may go to different churches, work in different ministries or have differing views on some doctrines, but all who have been born of the Spirit are members of one body, one family. We belong to one another in the most profound relationship, and that's why Paul urges us to "keep the unity of the Spirit through the bond of peace."[9]

The door is open for us to go through at any

time, in any circumstance of life, communicating directly with the One who spoke the worlds into existence. He invites us to pray, and we do so with adoration, with confession, with petition, with thanksgiving, and—very importantly—with intercession for one another.

7

GIVING THE GIFT OF LOVE

Putting First the Thing That Matters Most

If the Bible were a door, what would be its hinges?

Believe it or not, Jesus answered this question when he was asked, "Teacher, which is the greatest commandment in the Law?" The man who posed the question was a lawyer whose intention was to entrap Jesus, provoking Him to say something the Pharisees could hold against Him. But, being infinitely wiser than his inquisitors, Jesus replied: "'Love the Lord your God with all your heart and with all your soul and with all your mind.' This is the first and greatest commandment." But He did not stop there. Jesus continued, "And the second is like it: 'Love your neighbor as yourself.'" And to top it off, He then made a remarkable summary statement: "All the Law and the Prophets hang on these two commandments."[1]

The entire Old Testament hangs on the hinges of these two commandments.

Jesus was saying categorically that the entire Old Testament hangs on the hinges of these two commandments. If you love the Lord your God completely and you love your neighbor sincerely, you are living by the essence of all biblical teaching. Amazing.

The Bible is clear in telling us that love is the greatest. It is the greatest quality. It is the greatest virtue. It is the greatest gift.

Nothing tops love. It is greater than eloquence, greater than knowledge, greater than faith, greater than sacrifice, greater than hope, greater than anything.

*"If I speak in the tongues of men and of angels,
but have not love, I am only a resounding gong or
a clanging cymbal. If I have the gift of prophecy
and can fathom all mysteries and all knowledge,
and if I have a faith that can move mountains,
but have not love, I am nothing. If I give all I pos-
sess to the poor and surrender my body to the
flames, but have not love, I gain nothing... And
now these three remain: faith, hope and love. But
the greatest of these is love."*[2]

Days before the traumatic events of His passion, Jesus said to His followers, "A new command I
give you: Love one another. As I have loved you, so
you must love one another. By this all men will know
that you are my disciples, if you love one another." [3]
Imagine what must have gone through their minds
when days later they thought about one phrase in particular: "*As I have loved you...*" No one had ever loved
them as Jesus had loved—selflessly, completely, sacrificially. And that's how they were to love one another!

A powerful proof that we are truly followers of Christ is the love we demonstrate for other Christians. Philosopher and theologian Francis Schaeffer said that this one thing—genuine love—is the true mark of the Christian, transcending everything else.

The evidence of a spiritually empowered life is described in a list of nine qualities in Galatians 5:22-23. "The fruit of the Spirit," it says, "is love, joy, peace, patience, kindness, goodness, faithfulness, gentleness and self-control." Leading the list is love, and many biblical scholars believe that love by itself is the "fruit of the Spirit" and all the other qualities are simply by-products of love. Looking at the Scriptures, it's hard to disagree with that conclusion. There is no joy without love, no peace without love, no patience without love, no other virtue without love.

What does love look like? The highest and best description is found in 1 Corinthians, chapter 13, a memorable, moving passage of Scripture that reads with poetic beauty.

"Love is patient, love is kind. It does not envy, it does not boast, it is not proud. It is not rude, it is not self-seeking, it is not easily angered, it keeps no record of wrongs. Love does not delight in evil but rejoices with the truth. It always protects, always trusts, always hopes, always perseveres. Love never fails. But where there are prophecies, they will cease; where there are tongues, they will be stilled; where there is knowledge, it will pass away. For we know in part and we prophesy in part, but when perfection comes, the imperfect disappears... Now we see but a poor reflection as in a mirror; then we shall see face to face. Now I know in part; then I shall know fully, even as I am fully known. And now these three remain: faith, hope and love. But the greatest of these is love."[4]

Love is patient. It enables us to endure difficult people and troubling situations with a longsuffering spirit.

Love is kind. It prompts us, even when we are

treated unkindly, to respond with the kindness and gentleness of Jesus.

Love does not envy. When we look at others who have more "success" or more of this world's wealth, love guards the heart, stifling the urge to envy. It makes us content with what we have rather than dissatisfied with what we don't have.

Love makes us content with what we have rather than dissatisfied with what we don't have.

Love does not boast. Since everything we have and everything we are is a gift of God's grace, love makes us realize that there is no sensible reason to brag about ourselves.

Love is not proud. Pride—self-absorption and complete disregard for God—is one of the ugliest of all human tendencies. It is the diametric opposite of love.

Love is not rude. It doesn't interfere, insult or step on others' feelings.

Love is not self-seeking. In an age of utter self-centeredness, it stands against the tide, putting concern for others ahead of one's own interests.

Love is not easily angered. It doesn't fly off the handle at the slightest discomfort or offense.

Love keeps no record of wrongs. It has no "little black book" hidden in the heart, archiving the faults, failings and sins of others.

Love does not delight in evil. It finds no joy or satisfaction in unwholesome behavior or Christless attitudes.

Love rejoices with the truth. It is genuinely pleased when truth prevails, when what's right is done.

Love always protects. Like a mother guarding her young child, love guards what is precious. It pro-

Love believes the best to the nth degree.

tects against unfair personal attacks, hurtful gossip about other people, or anything that is counter to what is right and just.

Love always trusts. It believes the best to the nth degree.

Love always hopes. It looks positively to the future even where there seems no logical reason for confidence or certainty.

Love always perseveres. It gives, but never gives up. It holds on, no matter what storms may threaten. In a friendship, it endures difficulties and disagreements. In a marriage, it hangs on in spite of differences that others would deem irreconcilable. In the experiences of life, it never loses its grip.

Love never fails. It ultimately wins out. It reaches the finish line regardless of pitfalls and obstacles along the path.

Love is the ultimate quality of the Giving Christian, the motivating power that drives us to do the right thing, say the right word, show the right attitude. Think back to the vignettes of people in this book...

What motivated Bono to share his faith in Christ?

What motivated M. A. Thomas to put up with beatings, imprisonments and harassment for the sake of Christ?

What motivated two of my children, Ashley and Matthew, to give up their jobs and risk it all to help the battered people of Sudan?

What motivated the believers of Macedonia to give generously in spite of their own poverty?

What motivated that man to pick up the phone and call his brother after 30 long years of silence?

What motivated Jesus to pray so passionately for His followers?

In every case, there is one underlying motivation: true, Christlike love. On all the gifts we give, this is the "wrapping paper"—the beautiful covering for everything we offer to God and to one another.

I encourage you: Be a Giving Christian. Give the gift of Truth to those who ask you the reason for your hope in Christ. Give the gift of Help to those who need your compassion and assistance. Give the gift of Service whenever and wherever you have the opportunity to use your abilities for the Master. Give the gift of Resources, wisely investing material blessings to benefit others. Give the gift of Strength to all who need your encouragement, all who would be empowered by your life. Give the gift of Prayer on behalf of the people for whom your intercession can make all the difference. And, above all, give the gift of Love, the gift that transcends all others in value and importance.

Preface

1 Acts 20:35

Chapter 1

1 Assayas, Michka. <u>Bono: In Conversation with Michka Assayas</u>. New York: Riverhead Press, 2005, page 205.

2 1 Peter 3:15

3 John 14:1-6

4 John 18:37-38

5 Matthew 12:30

6 Romans 6:23

Chapter 2

1 Galatians 5:22

2 John 6:60

3 Ephesians 4:15

4 Matthew 9:36 (KJV)

5 Acts 10:2-4

Chapter 3

1 Ephesians 5:15-17

Chapter 4

1 Acts 20:35

2 2 Corinthians 9:7

3 John 3:16

4 1 Timothy 5:8

5 Haggai 1:4

6 Psalm 24:1

7 1 Corinthians 4:2

8 Matthew 6:21

9 Romans 8:32

10 Luke 12:48 (KJV)

11 2 Corinthians 8:1-5

12 Acts 1:8

13 John 3:16

14 Matthew 10:8

Chapter 5

1 Ecclesiastes 4:9

2 Matthew 14:25-31

3 Hebrews 10:24 (KJV)

Chapter 6

1 James 5:16
2 John 17:3
3 John 17:11
4 John 17:15
5 John 17:13
6 John 17:17
7 John 17:20
8 John 17:23
9 Ephesians 4:3

Chapter 7

1 Matthew 22:36-39
2 1 Corinthians 13:1-3, 13
3 John 13:34
4 1 Corinthians 13:4-13